15 Years of the Abbey Line Community Rail Partnership

By Paul Spelzini

A potted history of the Abbey Line Community rail partnership since its inception, its successes and missed opportunities; several political hiatuses and the present-day situation with a look toward the future.

Written and compiled by Paul Spelzini c/o the Abbey Line Community Rail partnership.

Contents;

1. Early Days

It was a cold, wet blustery January day in 2004 when I recall I first met Maria Cutler then of Herts County Council (now St. Albans district council) at St. Albans Abbey station to progress the idea of forming a 'Community rail partnership' for the Abbey Line.

The Community Rail partnership was initially to consist of Hertfordshire County Council who would fund a part time officer and some support staff via the Passenger Transport Unit and others, including a rail officer; Network Rail, The Train Operating Franchisee, St. Albans District Council, Watford Borough Council, St. Stephen's Parish Council, the BRE and CAMRA.

Other organisations including ACORP and the DOT were represented later or for certain periods

The Abbey Line was a 6.5-mile long single-track branch line operating every 45 minutes approximately and using old class 421 electric multiple unit trains cascaded from Great Eastern and elsewhere.

The line was operated at that time by Silver link, a National Express franchise which was due to expire in 2007 and was subsequently not renewed.

At that time Silver link services appeared run down and their network did not have a particularly good reputation for reliability, especially on their north London lines which are now part of London Overground.

A windswept and bleak abbey station at the CRP's inception

The fledgling ACORP which oversees community rail partnerships was in consultation with the government and giving initial advice and guidance on setting up of proposed groups.

Initially there were some 55 groups nationwide, of which the Abbey Line was one of 6 initial pilots to promote best practice and new ideas concerning the operation of run down and rural and branch lines in the UK.

A small group was set up at Watford North on the line, which was the first station adoption group, and heralded a new start with much fanfare. This included the original adopters who have since retired.

Sadly, over the years we have lost many adopters for various reasons, and several have passed away like John Webster, the inaugural CRP chairman.

Handing over the CRP chair to HCC in March 2009 with John Webster and Jane, the 2nd CRP officer (now HCC rail officer) in attendance

At the Abbey, Jack Hill and myself formed the first adoption group for the end of the line, but there was a gap between Watford North and the Abbey with no-one initially covering this.

After a year or so, I agreed to cover Park Street, How Wood and Bricket Wood with John from North Watford also covering Garston, now covered by David Nursaw.

Jack did the Abbey until recently, but Jack is now in his 90's and unable to do this role anymore.

Watford Junction was always a bit of a misnomer as a mainline station, as it was covered by John in theory, but the TOC tended to use the displays for their own purposes.

ABFLY were the train user group already established on the line, run by the charismatic John Webster.

However, ABFLY's aims were not always the same at the CRP's and this led to a spectacular falling out in the teens when HCC as chair of the CRP proposed a rapid bus link for the Abbey Line which ABFLY and residents flatly rejected.

ABFLY then promptly left the CRP for approximately 3 years between 2015/16 and late 2018.

ABFLY also were a lobbying group and pressed for line improvements including better fare collection which was distorting usage figures; a passing loop and more frequent service and peak through service to Euston.

A Silver link plaque celebrating 140 years of the 'Abbey Flyer'

My initial input was to produce a sketch plan for the Abbey station to clean up the overgrown jungle that adjoined the car park.

Network Rail did some tree pruning, but it was countryside management that eventually cleared the embankment, which was proposed as a tactile garden, seating area and coffee shop originally.

We did have a containerised coffee shop for several years, but it proved unsuccessful as it was only busy during the morning peak. The tactile garden concept got lost somewhere in negotiations between the TOC and Network Rail which was a real shame.

2. Silver link

Silver link were the Train operating company running services on the Abbey Line between 2004 and 2007 when London Midland were awarded the franchise on 12th December.

The Abbey line operated the first ever London Midland train, but it was a diesel service due to engineering work affecting the main line overhead electrics.

An early CRP event with John Webster, former chair in the foreground

Maria, our first CRP officer lasted a year of so before leaving to join St. Albans District Council. We then had our second CRP officer who also did not last long, deciding to switch within Herts county council to become rail officer instead.

So, within 2 years of the Community rail partnership being formed, we were onto our 3rd CRP officer, as Herts County Council ran the CRP initially with a part time appointment, so there was little promotion initially.

It was hoped the CRP would pilot new ideas and there was much discussion about a passing loop. This was investigated and costed by Network Rail but came out very expensive.

A report was prepared looking into tram operation as an alternative, and even got as far as a draft bill to allow this to happen, but sadly did not proceed either.

A CGI of a passing loop at Bricket Wood that ABFLY have campaigned for

In the early days of the CRP, the partnership would hold 2 events a year in conjunction with Silver link, usually an 'Easter Eggspress' and a Santa Special.

These days, that has translated into a fun day in May and a Santa Special.

When Silver link lost their franchise, some of the CRP events were lost temporarily so we had no Santa specials for several years, plus during the 'hiatus' periods of 2009/10 and 2013/4 when there appeared to be no-one in charge.

Indeed, the CRP was effectively a small 'band of brothers' of adopters who just kept going with little or no support when all seemed lost.

Somehow, they managed to maintain a respectable semblance of order and posters were maintained to reassure the public and ABFLY that the CRP hadn't died prematurely.

The future of the CRP itself was very much in doubt when Herts County Council were looking to offload responsibility for running it and funding the CRP officers' position.

The Silver link era was not particularly notable for its achievements, but the CRP debate nationwide had started, and the Abbey Line started winning things at national level, much to their own surprise initially. The CRP has also achieved 4 further nominations and commendations which is very laudable.

This was due to their vision and marketing strategies and idea of Carnet tickets introduced by Geraint Thomas, which was sadly short lived, and getting schools involved in CRP activities.

Silver link's crowning glory was ironically as they signed off on their franchise, when they decided one year to host a ghost train at Halloween.

Silver link's ghost train - one of the scariest rides on the Abbey line ever!

Some 450 very excited children and adults all turned up with adults in fancy dress one Saturday evening in the dark, and it turned out to be arguably the greatest public relations success that the CRP and Silver link had ever had.

Silver link decorated the whole train like a chamber of horrors, and it was the scariest ride ever from the photos. Children locally talked about it for weeks afterwards right up to Christmas I recall.

Silver link finally signed off with their trademark Santa specials with Geoff Harrison acting as Santa, as he has done for many years, with Silver link staff as elves, with face painters and Rotary helping.

So, although Silver link had a mixed reception from rail users and the CRP, they were oddly fondly remembered for kick starting a chain of events involving the passing loop, station refurbishments, and upgrading the line in general.

Geoff Harrison plays the role of Santa for Silver link's swansong

3. The 2010-12 and 2013/4 Hiatuses.

Maria Cutler was the first Abbey Line CRP officer from 2005, until Jane took over briefly before becoming rail officer for the county. Alissa Ede was next, stepping up for the 150th anniversary of the line in 2008 and she lasted until circa 2009.

Part of the problem for the adopters at the time was that we were submitting reports to what we thought was the CRP officer; when in fact they were sometimes going to different departments at County hall such as the Passenger Transport Unit or even HCC Highways?

Community rail Officers were also appointed on a probationary basis so that some were often 'acting' Community rail officers, like Jane with no permanent contract. So of course, they got a better offer from elsewhere and promptly left.

Alissa Ede lasted until 2009 but then there was approximately a year with no Community rail partnership officer in post. Adopters such as yours truly continued compiling reports and had to cover for people who were no longer there or had moved to cover other stations?

The 3rd CRP officer Alissa Ede at the 150th line celebrations in Watford, August 2008 at the launch of the special Abbey Line beer.

This was a confusing situation not knowing who to report to or indeed not knowing who was in control at any given time.

This was a time of political change at County hall, with proposals flying around about passing loops and converting the line to a guided busway.

That infuriated ABFLY, the rail user group who subsequently quit the CRP for approximately 3 years between 2015/16 and late 2018.

Eventually John Gunner was appointed as CRP officer-the only man to have held the post funnily enough. He was an affable man and very popular with all adopters alike.

He was actively involved from around 2010 although his initial appointment was not confirmed for some time. He stayed with the CRP until around 2012 but sadly later died, becoming the first CRP officer to have passed away.

We also lost John Webster by 2015 so several key personnel in the CRP disappeared around this time.

Sadly, there are very few known pictures of John Gunner which a shame is as he was fondly remembered by my late daughter. She was one of the early adopters, and they got on like a house on fire.

I remember Fran making a video about using the Abbey Line as a media project at John's suggestion.

CRP boards were kept up to date despite no-one being in post officially

He was replaced by a lady called Janet Stevens who was in post for a year or so, but then defected to South Eastern after the adopters' Christmas dinner in St. Albans at

Christmas one year, leaving a gap in the CRP for a further year or two.

Herts County Council seemed in no rush to fill the post due to increasing financial pressures and it was not seen as a priority at that time; so, adopters carried on with business as usual, although with no co-ordination (or funding) for a while.

The hiatus continued until eventually Herts County Council relinquished control of the CRP to the present incumbent, and Edna Wonome was appointed and continues to act as the public face of the CRP officer today.

The CRP though was transferred to a new body acting together with Beds RCC acting out of Watford BC's offices rather than County Hall.

The hiatus had finally been ended but at a cost. We had lost many original adopters along the way who had either retired or didn't think the CRP was continuing as there had been little progress for such a long time.

It is important to remember that the CRP officer is the only paid appointment in the local Community Rail setup.

The adopters and volunteers all act voluntarily at CRP events, even though they may be employed by the Train Operating Company or other rail organisations such as Network Rail.

A photograph of the original abbey line adopters who kept the Abbey line CRP spirit alive, seen here on a visit to our sister CRP line at Marston Vale on 24th July 2012.

4. London Midland

London Midland won the franchise to take over from Silver link on Sunday 12th December straight after Silver link's Abbey Line Santa Specials.

The initial weeks and months saw little change with Alissa Ede as our CRP officer, but the preparations were building towards the grand 150th celebrations that summer on 8th August.

However, stations along the line started to see overhaul and modernisation which took some years to complete fully, transforming an ageing branch line into a modern railway system.

The first ever London Midland train seen at a misty Abbey, December 2008

The 150th celebrations were to be elaborate, with a parade in St. Albans city centre, Network rail's robot on show at Bricket Wood, public displays and events including a fun day at the Abbey.

There was also a CAMRA beer brewed specially for the occasion which is now a collectors' item; and a specially commissioned theatre show at the Abbey Theatre.

The weather held and all went well on the day.

London Midland rebranded the existing 421 class trains on the line but there were rumours of new trains, and sure enough class 350's appeared on the main line.

London Midland did try a class 350 on the Abbey Line, but said the clearances were too tight and limited stop running to a tighter timetable proved difficult in practice.

The CRP arranged a visit to the Watford signal box as there were considerable engineering works around this time lasting several years.

This involved some unusual visitors to the Abbey Line, including a class 66 weed killer train in the dead of night. A very rare sight.

The very rare class 66 weed killer train taken in the dead of night at the Abbey.

Chartered trains on the Abbey line were often requested by ABFLY but usually refused by Network rail, but with one notable exception.

In November 2011, Spitfire rail tours planned a rail tour to all branch lines in southern England, including the Abbey Line.

The last scheduled train was then at 2150, so it had to arrive after that time, when the line had been vacated and cleared by the signal man.

It arrived at 23.00 with large crowds of day trippers visiting the Abbey line for the first time. It was unusual sight-seeing Southern buffet cars and first-class Midland dining cars at the Abbey station in Southern green and Midland red colours.

Class 37 685 seen at the Abbey late one Saturday night 23rd October 2011 on a Spitfire Rail tours special

London Midland's first real challenge was to organise the 150th line celebrations in August 2008. This involved a big effort on the part of all, including local authorities, the CRP, Rail operator and local interests such as BRE and CAMRA.

The day itself was on a Sunday, and Network Rail's robot was on show at Bricket Wood. There was a parade in St. Albans, a fun day at the Abbey and events in Watford also.

There was a launch of a special beer brewed for the occasion, and a specially commissioned play at the Abbey Theatre depicting 150 years in traditional dress.

The special 150ᵗʰ play at the Abbey Theatre; celebrating 150 years of the Abbey line in August 2008.

London Midland also were fast introducing new trains and sprucing up stations.

There was a marked improvement in poster cases and publicity which previously was using leaky stained old cases.

These became modern standard cases with a standard key, as many of the old cases had odd keys which was a pain for adopters and TOC alike.

Except during the hiatuses, when there were no events around 2014/5; the CRP reverted to 2 events a year in the summer and winter, with the Santa specials and fun day restarting during 2015/16.

There was also a photo competition which I won around 2011 depicting the 'essence of the Abbey Line' when we had an Arctic winter and blizzards, with Santa special users boarding a train in thick snow that year.

Winning picture from ABFLY's photo competition of the 'Essence of the Abbey Line' taken during the Santa Special in a blizzard in December 2011.

Meanwhile ABFLY had fallen out with Herts county council and operated independently of them until re-joining the CRP recently.

The CRP organised joint visits with our sister CRP at Marston Vale including a trip on the Marston vale line up to Ridgemont; and a trip to Bletchley Park for a seminar.

One interesting point that London Midland did was to introduce a flexible multi-storey car parking system at stations to match changing demand.

This saw a multi-storey car park deck removed from Bletchley where there was static demand, to Leighton Buzzard and Tring where demand was increasing at that time.

London Midland also introduced car park charges at the Abbey and Watford Junction which compared unfavourably with the City station at weekends, although car parks at Bricket Wood and Park Street were privately owned.

The CRP's purpose was to promote the Abbey Line, and indeed it was not until a fare review recently that numbers using the Abbey Line changed significantly.

The line saw a decline during the recession but has bounced back to around half a million users since.

However, the big change occurred partly down to the World cup and partly down to standardising fares with Thameslink to London, which was the Abbey Line's biggest direct competitor for rail traffic.

Peak or standard fares were comparable at circa £20 return for both lines, but Thameslink were charging just £8 return to London compared to the Abbey Line charging nearly £13-19 for a similar journey.

It was not until more promotional fares were introduced that we saw some passenger shift in numbers at weekends particularly during the World Cup by 2018, when London North Western had taken over the Franchise.

Rail fares were also undercutting bus fares which rose during this period, so the Abbey line was winning some new custom from failing parallel off-peak bus routes such as the 652 (now 361).

There were also deep county bus cuts at weekends and evenings in 2015 which saw a rise in line usage at these times.

London Midland also introduced a late evening weekday service for commuters and sports/ leisure users which has Watford fans during midweek games, gaining an average of 80 new customers since.

London Midland also set up close ties with Samaritans to reduce rail casualties which was successful, with poster campaigns at Abbey and other stations.

Very poignant following the death of my late daughter and Abbey line adopter Fran to Schizophrenia in 2009. I now wear a green ribbon in her memory.

London Midland also saw the introduction of an SC1 DoT funded 1-year bus contract to link the Abbey and City stations in St. Albans for rail travellers.

This gained 19,800 passengers in its first year, and the contract was extended 2 months, but the service was discontinued for lack of funding despite being popular with users.

London Midland also introduced some better connections with mainline services although connections with Southern's vital Croydon-Milton Keynes service that I use a lot are still very hit and miss.

The debate over a passing loop, bus rapid transit or tram service rumbled on since 2011 but eventually failed due to too many logistical problems.

By late 2017 it was confirmed London Midland had lost their franchise with some unfulfilled commitments. These included a smart card for the Abbey Line, as Oyster had been operational south of Watford Junction since 2008.

We said goodbye to London Midland, but they had transformed the Abbey line into a modern rail route over their 10-year stay, and we are grateful for that.

New lighting installed at all stations made a real difference in reducing crime

5. London and North Western Railway

London and North Western railway are the current incumbent train operating company for the Abbey Line, effectively since December 2018.

However, planning for the changeover had been in place for a year or so previously.

The new franchisee was promising some new trains for the Abbey Line, a smart card system like Oyster called Swift card, operational initially in the West Midlands, and other sundry promised line improvements.

We had a visit to the Severn Valley railway last summer for adopters nationally across the West Midlands network at Kidderminster and Bridge-north, which was a nice day travelling on steam trains in bright sunshine with scenic countryside.

West Midlands Trains station adopters gathered at Kidderminster

I was also invited up to Glasgow for the ACORP annual awards in October 2018, but sadly ALCRP failed to continue their trick of winning a steady stream of awards since around 2008.

These were for such things including marketing initiatives, getting school children involved in the line, artwork and promoting walking trails along the line.

Sadly, my award entry for 2017 of depicting the line history in thumbnail photos was disqualified on a technicality which was frustrating. Hopefully the book version will fare better.

Our sister line, Marston Vale fared better winning the photo competition via their talisman, Stephen Sleight.

Its probably too early to judge how the new franchisee is doing, but there are signs of new timetable and fare initiatives which are welcome.

That is after public complaints that cheap £5-10 fares were being widely offered and promoted from London to Birmingham and Liverpool.

The peak fare from Abbey station to Birmingham on the same network was approximately £189 at one time which was completely unaffordable for most normal people.

London and North Western have introduced through trains from Walsall and Rugeley to London, so it is hoped that one day we can have through trains to Euston once again.

That may be after HS2 phase 1 is operational in 2026, when there is spare line capacity on the west coast main line.

Community Fun day at the Abbey Station 2018

6. The future for the Abbey Line Community Rail partnership

The Community Rail partnership concept has proved popular since its inception, and is now more secure than originally, when funding sources were scarce.

One of the great frustrations with the Abbey Line CRP is that Network Rail have effectively stage-managed projects, so that adopters are effectively excluded.

We tried to implement a tactile garden at the Abbey station for deaf and blind people in 2008, but were told that the train operator does not own the forecourt verges, and adopters were not insured to do projects on their own?

So, we looked on enviously at other CRPs such as the Bittern Lines CRP; where they had opened a coffee and bookshop, introduced widespread planting and other nice features.

Some CRP have their own offices now, which would be great, as we had suggested a tourist office or pop up shop in the city to promote tourism.

It is perhaps ironic that even the mighty Amazon are now proposing 'pop up' retail units after virtually wiping out the retail market? There are plenty of vacant ones in St. Albans.

St. Albans tourism now effectively operates out of a cupboard and small room in the Civic Centre which is hard to find for tourists.

A smart card seems a certainty in the immediate future; with ticket machines, like cash machines, becoming largely redundant eventually.

The London North Western Smartcard

Newer trains are a possibility, and we also anticipate that the Bricket Wood building will eventually become a CRP office/ display space/ café subject to planning consents.

The roof is currently being extensively repaired where the building has been disused for over a decade.

The CRP itself will probably continue to be funded as now via Beds CC and/ or commercial sponsorship and operate out of Watford's council offices.

However, things can change and sometimes do. The CRP officer's position is part-time but seems to have expanded to 4 days a week from 3 due to increasing workload and more projects.

The main project that could affect the Abbey Line is the A414 Park Street or St. Albans South hub as it is known.

This is a project to make the A414 corridor multi modal, introducing cycle and footpaths, a possible MRT system which seems very unlikely given that HCC can't even fund existing bus services adequately, and a park and ride with the City station from the A414 and relocated Park Street station.

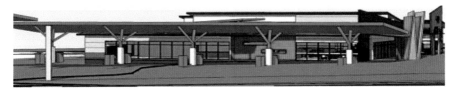

A CGI of the proposed solar powered Park Street Hub.

The scheme would involve relocating or extending Park Street station up to the A414 trunk road, building a sustainable 'Grass-Crete' car park for park and ride passengers, a Bailey bridge across the A414 to link the Sop well area including the busy Sop well House Hotel and Conference Centre, Blacks and small business park which gets no bus service at all.

This would continue up Cotton mill lane to London Road, turn right to serve the wonderfully refurbished Odyssey cinema, then left down Alma Road to City station.

The abbey shuttle bus formerly linking the city and abbey stations

Funnily enough an old road sign for the previous defunct park and ride scheme still exists on the A414 and is now some 25+ years old.

This scheme could potentially take traffic out of the city and provide new bus links to the city station and city for rail travellers and locals alike.

It would be a welcome change from traffic speeds at a 20mph crawl, giving cyclists priority instead of pedestrians and not making the most of the Abbey Line's inherent advantages.

This scheme may involve some novel ticketing such as a bus/rail through ticket or bus plus for both stations.

Online ticketing is also expected to become the norm so that conventional cash and BR orange card style ticketing could eventually die out.

The CRP started out with a branch line, but could end up with a fully electrified suburban rail route into London like Hertford East, given time?

A Southern through service from Platform 10 to Croydon, adjacent the Abbey line. Perhaps one day Abbey line trains will run through to Euston once again?

About the Author;

Paul was 62 at the time of writing this book, and married for over 30 years with 3 children, 3 grandchildren; and an Old English sheepdog puppy.

Paul is a Chartered Surveyor and Engineer by training, with over 40 years' experience.

He is also a voluntary station adopter with the Abbey Line Community rail partnership since its inception in 2004/5; and has run a voluntary local transport user group since 1986.

He is also a leading UK flight and traditional archer.

Paul has written published and self-published books plus various published technical articles on planning and development.

*If you enjoyed reading this book, then perhaps you may enjoy reading other books by the same author;

Planning and Development-Changing the way we travel;

An Express Bus Network for Hertfordshire Business

30 Years of Bus Deregulation

My Wonderful Fran

Artificial Nocturne

@#1Crush

END

Printed in Great Britain
by Amazon

59743556R20024